HOW TO BECOME A GOOD TEAM LEADER AND A SUPERVISOR AND EARN THE RESPECT

A REALISTIC AND PRACTICAL LOOK
AT THE WAY IT IS DONE EFFECTIVELY;
UNIONISED OR NOT.

TR.SABRA

DEDICATION
To My Father

TABLE OF CONTENTS

- INTRODUCTION...05

- CHAPTER 1
- How to lead your TEAM........10

- CHAPTER 2
- How to relate with your BOSS....40

- CHAPTER 3
- How to relate with other SUPERVISORS...52

- CHAPTER 4
- DOS AND DON'TS...64

This book is a must-read for you: If you are a new or young supervisor and you have never led a team before. If you are an experienced supervisor but would like to sharpen your tools. No knowledge gained is wasted, especially not knowledge that hits the nail on the head!

INTRODUCTION

LEADERSHIP

Constant, gentle pressure is my preferred technique for leadership, guidance and coaching.

Danny Meyer

I know that you have criticized a previous supervisor and thought that being one was easy; however, if you have ever had to be one- you'd have discovered that it seems more challenging than you thought it was. Supervision requires a hefty dose of leadership, a healthy balance of practicality, and a tool-box of "people skills."

Before we go deep into the formal requirements of becoming a good supervisor, let's define who a supervisor is, shall we?

A "supervisor" is a front-line team leader who can perform multiple tasks such as directing, coaching, rewarding, and delegating. A supervisor is additionally responsible for his department's productivity, staff safety, and daily tasks completion.

Previously, supervisors had to gradually climb the ladder to progress from a clerk to foreman than to a supervisor, accumulating experience and knowledge that leads to the position. However, when "Unions" drew the line between workers and management, it became progressively harder to elevate those few experienced workers (who now don't want to leave the "Union" fear of losing their seniority) to the supervisory position. This situation resulted in supervisors hired from the outside bypassing the years and tears of earning that position but lacking the proper knowledge to fill those shoes. They are now on the floor learning what the company sells and the process of production, and at the same time, supervising employees who have more experience in the field.

The employees are adjusted to the company's norms and can speak the company's vocabulary better than the new and fresh supervisor. So, how can the new supervisor earn their respect in this situation? I know, I've been there. It's very tough to look professional and assume what you are doing when everyone knows you don't.

As a new supervisor, you are second-guessing every step of the way, and the simple truth is that it is challenging to walk in those shoes.

From your first day on the job, you will face new challenges. You have never been on the spot like this before. And for many like you, the few articles or books you've read on the subject and the "how-to videos" you watched on YouTube have been barely enough to prepare you for what was coming.

Just a blatant dependence on character and other life experiences is not enough. In my opinion, in the modern era, many young people are untrained in communication skills, mostly due to the virtual "social network" habits that left most individuals without any real social interaction with real people.

Instead, we have individuals who are one-click away from everything, instead of having "face to face "or "eye to eye" contact with real people. Even some who claim to have limited experience with supervision and who have managed a few teenagers at a coffee shop will find it challenging to face and lead a massive factory population and endure the atmosphere. An atmosphere of giant machines roaring all night, with industrial vehicles driving by, and union reps waiting for you to make a mistake- in the middle of the graveyard shift.

So how do you expect someone who has never interacted much with "real" people, let alone challenged a real person in his life, to fare in a sea of unsatisfied employees and angry bosses?

This book targets this exact audience—the new supervisor without any experience in leading people and whom leadership thrust into their hands, and the old supervisor who has the enviable experience yet seeking guidance on tweaking his or her game and getting better at the job.

This book is for you!

As a supervisor, you must deal with unmotivated people and lead them towards finishing the tasks they have on hand consistently. You are also dealing with equally essential elements such as; machines, schedules, safety, and decision making. You must be aware of many things at once; you have to carry the big picture in your head to contain the situation and deal with it.

Furthermore, you have to report, listen, communicate, and take directives from your boss, regardless of whether you like him/her or not. You are the shock absorber of the company and the link between different levels. Therefore, If you feel insecure and not ready in your role. If you lack leadership skills as well as the openness to take and give directives. If you've never challenged or directed anybody to do anything for you. This book will then show you how to do so and help you with the skill set needed to achieve it.

After all, you don't want to feel frustrated at the end of your working day, and you don't want to feel like "not coming" back to work the next morning.

This book will show you how you respond to most situations, even if you think in a certain way; there is the supervisor's way.

This book has fewer pages because it goes straight to the point and because I was hoping you could read it as many times as possible. In big companies, Government Corporations, the supervisor is working in a unionized environment. The employees are mostly assembly line workers who need constant motivation; their job is "monotone" and demanding, and your job as their supervisor is very demanding too. Your superiors are also very demanding; this means that if you are not ready, and if you are not reliable enough, and if you are not flexible enough, they will break you. But you will not let them. You are reading this book. You are going to establish your name, and you are going to earn your respect. You are going to be firm and flowing at the same time. This book will show you how to practically and efficiently carry out the job, deal with your employees, your boss, and the other supervisors, behave under stress, and above all, maintain the upper hand and earn your RESPECT.

TR. Sabra

CHAPTER 1

HOW TO LEAD YOUR TEAM

WORK

> *The reason factories are prosperous is
> that there is no place to sit down.*
>
> *American Proverb*

IN THE BEGINNING

After working in the same company for years, you become very comfortable and familiar with your job. You feel like you know the ropes; the daily routine becomes like second-nature, and the level of understanding of what you are doing becomes very high.

Nevertheless, as soon as you take a step forward in your career from being the clerk to become the supervisor, your daily efforts will change from basically "physical" to frequently "mental." And if you are not ready for what is coming, you are in for a ride, a very shaky one! Because while time cures physical stress, mental stress takes longer to fade.

When you worked as a clerk for years, you had 8 hours a day to yourself in your mental bubble. You rarely had any disturbance to your peace of mind; you were completely relaxed in that position. And maybe you were even allowed to listen to music while carrying your job. You were yourself most of the time. No one personally ever seriously challenged you, blamed you, or even questioned you for a significant mishap— and most importantly, no one personally named "you" as "the" responsible for the daily outcome. Your mental muscles were weak and completely numb; it had barely any training or any challenges, and for years, you were walking freely with your guard down and not prepared for retaliation from any kind. Now, however, things are about to change radically. As a supervisor, things will be completely different.

I want you to think about your decisions and plan your every move, but first, you have to change, and you have to become a new person.

When you go to work, "GO to work."

This one has nothing to do with your attendance, although your attendance is essential and discussed later.

When you go to work every day, it must be crystal clear in your head to be present with all your senses and ultimately knowing your purpose in your job. You are there to fulfill a duty and to achieve an objective.

Do you remember when you applied for the job and felt extremely lucky to be given the job?

So, you were very excited then! You even vowed to yourself that you would put your best foot forward each day of your stay within the organization and several other lofty promises. It is also very possible that they chose you for this job because you were the most suitable candidate for the job, having gone up in rankings throughout your company.

For that, you sacrificed years of seniority to do just this, and of course, for a better salary and a higher status. Therefore, you do not have the luxury of being lax about the job you ought to perform; you have to roll up those sleeves and work, wear the mask and transform, and become the boss! You can relax at home later, but when you come to work, work, and give it all you have got.

The company's success depends on you, and your superiors count on you as they have been in your shoes before and got promoted to a higher level.

So stop wishing you were somewhere else, take charge of your job and your duty, and stop anticipating how stressful your day will be.

The ultimate objective is always to remain focused.

A few years back, we had a supervisor who comes to work and relax. To him, the driven, motivated, and task-performing supervisors were a joke and "running for nothing." Eventually, he got into the habit of procrastination, and the work began piling up; he lost control, lost the floor, and lost the trust of everyone around him—why? Because he was not ready and not on the ball. He was so incapable that when the boss asked him a simple question, he would give any reply, and then he started to tell lies to cover up his tracks. Eventually, this man got fired, and I dare say he deserved it.

As Jim Rohn said, "Life is one of two pains, the pain of preparing and working hard or that of losing, you choose." The discomfort of always being alert and focused is more comfortable than the grief of losing out, losing your respect, your credibility, and eventually, your job.

Your boss and, above all, your employees have to feel your presence, they have to be confident in your ability as the leader, and then you become that person everyone looks up to and wants to respect. Do not disappoint them.

Establish your reputation first.

In the beginning, you should remain serious and respect the company's rules to the letter, and for as long as you can. Remember that you have to establish your reputation first. You have to make a name for yourself of being a serious-by the book-person. Everyone has to know you by that first, and then, you can become yourself. Being blunt and by the book does not mean that you should not be "understanding" or "humane," but it means that before the "Flexibility" in decision-making, you have to make a signature for yourself first. You have to be: bold, just, and capable, capable of all options, but you can choose the friendlier option whenever you see fit. It should be clear for everyone that before you make that "exception," you have a long-standing history of being determined, fair, and just.

Furthermore, before you "let it go this time," you must also have had a history of applying accountability across the board.

Before you have paid for your staff's lunch as a gesture of appreciation, it should be clear to your team that it is "their job" to do the work with or without lunch.

Your role is not to bribe them for the work to be done; it is to supervise them and ensure that they carry out the work. The company pays their salary.

As much as the words "friend or nice" sounds positive, my advice to you is that it would be best if you did not get carried away with being "the nice boss." Be friendly but not friends.

What to do?

Do what is expected of you to do: CONFRONTATIONS.

It is not unusual to find many new supervisors being particularly avoidant of confrontations and hoping that situations will resolve themselves. It is also tempting to turn a blind eye to slower productivity or to any conflict among your staff and expect somebody to solve it later magically.

New supervisors and people in general, try to avoid:

- Accusing to people's faces.
- Asking a "serious question."
- Handing out "violation letter or ticket."
- Blaming someone to his face for "loss or failure."

And it is incredibly hard for the "extra-friendly" supervisor to do so; his easy-going-funny personality is already stripped from every bit of seriousness, credibility, and power. So how do you expect him to shift back to respect?

Again, be friendly but not friends; you don't want to be "the nice guy."

You should know that it is tough to be serious with your friends, and it is ineffective to question a person you have a crush on, and it is challenging for you to be taken seriously if most of what comes of your mouth are jokes. Take your emotions out of your job, and stay professional.

That is why it is crucial to separate yourself from your staff and stay a notch professionally higher, and never get intimately involved with anyone nor extra friendly.

Do your job!.

In case of disputes, you should always intervene and do not hope that all will go away; offenders will NOT stop independently without intervention. Sorry to burst your bubble, dear new supervisor, It is called your job for a reason, and your presence is needed when issues present itself. You do not get to turn a blind eye to these issues! You must be well aware of the laws set down by your company, and you should apply these laws to the letter, as long as there are rules.

Remember, you are not there to harass people yourself; you are there to do what is expected of you to do – it is your job.

Before you become a supervisor, you must be very ready for confrontations; if you are not, those present when infringements on company rule in your presence but without any decent intervention will judge you as incapable and ineffective. It would be best if you do not avoid it, but you should not escalate it either. Confrontations and the way you handle and the adequate dosage you use are the regulators for your respect-o meter.

One day, I replaced a supervisor on vacation for a couple of weeks in a department of 20 employees; their lunch break was at 11:30 am. However, this group of employees stopped working by 11:15, 15 minutes before the actual time, and started slowing down significantly. More than half of them were in the washrooms with 4-5 employees in the cafeteria already. I had to do something because a pure loss of 15 minutes multiplied by 20 employees is a considerable loss to any company's standards, which means money loss.

I was perturbed by it that the next day I brought it up in our early morning meeting. I explained my concerns about their early departure to lunch and laid down a "rule" -everyone who repeats this offense to get a written warning and an eventual "consequence" from that day onward. During my speech, one person said: "but we have been doing it for months, and the other supervisor did not say anything."

"So why are you bringing it up now?"

I explained my productivity formula and the time loss calmly, and then I said "jokingly" that we are all paid by the hour and not by the three-quarters of an hour, and then I finished my phrase with a straight face saying: This is the rule, and from now on, I expect everyone to do just that.

I encountered rejection, discontent; but I made my point clear and straightforward. On the same day, everyone stayed working until 11:30, as I told them, except for three who were indifferent to what I asked for that morning and have left for lunch early. When the lunch break was over, I handed the discipline notices to the three in front of everyone unapologetically. I confronted them and told them that what they have done is unacceptable and unfair for the company and disrespectful to their co-workers and me.
By facing it, it was the only way to establish order! If you do not confront bad-practices, no one will.

As soon as the other supervisor came back from his vacation, I told him what happened, and indeed, he had heard what happened from them. I told him to take advantage of my actions and to maintain control. He thanked me and said: "It was difficult to talk to them about it because everyone was doing it because of a previous supervisor who was also, Not-too-strict."

It was an inheritance of bad behavior that went unchallenged for a long time, and someone had to do something about it.

WHO IS A SUPERVISOR?

A supervisor is the army officer in the field; he is the police officer on duty, and he is the school's principal telling little kids not to fight in the playground. As long as these professionals cannot go a day at work without confrontations, you also cannot.

Take the police for a model: The police force is vital to society in every way, and an officer who turns a blind eye to drivers speeding or crossing a red light just because he or she does not like confrontations is not an officer. A police officer faces daily: begging, shouting, lying, and denying; aggression and evasion, but still, and despite all of that, he has to do what he is supposed to do; that is his job.

A supervisor is expected and required to act.

Imagine yourself looking at a police officer, granting those offenders to go without even a warning. Forget respect; just the thought that the streets will turn into a jungle is enough motive to get a police officer going.

This officer's job is to confront and restrain offenders by handing tickets or even arresting them if the situation requires.

Everyone is expecting him or her to play this role despite the severe discontent of the population. Hence, everyone expects you to do your job as a supervisor too, or your workplace may lose control and lose business, and everyone may lose their job as a consequence.

So you have to change, and you have to adapt to a different character and become a new person.

I remember my first year as a supervisor; my wife complained about I becoming more argumentative and controlling at home. I could not let things pass like before. Moreover, I became very blunt and straight forward. I am not proud of it now, but I had to comment on everything; I became very opinionated back then. It became my mindset as I was changing my character at work. Even my friends noticed it. Effortlessly, I became the pack leader, commanding them whenever we went out and always choosing for the group. However, luckily I gradually adjusted to knowing the difference and where I was.

Your involvement is expected.

Two employees almost engaged in a "boxing" fight when a supervisor stood between them passively.

He was trying to block them from each other physically, while they were both insulting and threatening each other for 5 minutes.

After everything had calmed down, he asked them to go back to their workstations, trying not to escalate the situation more than it was. As the two finally calmed down, they both went back to work, and the supervisor thought that he has succeeded in resolving a big problem. Nevertheless, he did not. The two individuals -who have not spoken to each other since the incident- saw me afterward and recounted to me what had happened.

While describing the event, both were notably amazed at how the supervisor was very patient and did not suspend them immediately or call security. Both were mentally prepared to be suspended from work, with no pay and on the spot from the fighting impact. However, no. Moreover, what stood in their memory is the lack of discipline on the supervisor's part. Yes, they were fighting and arguing, but in their subconscious mind, they held the thought of the possibility of getting fired or suspended, the chance of losing a well-paid job and a career, a pension plan, for stupidity.

Any fight with any co-worker is not essential in front of getting fired and losing a livelihood. That supervisor did not apply what they were expecting him to do, "although they were thankful for his non-reaction."

However, deep inside, they were aware that someone else would have solved the situation in a different, consequential way.

With his non-confrontational behavior, that supervisor lost control, and employees felt free to disrespect each other. There were many individual conflicts in his department, and he had the most fights among employees and the most complaints.

The energy and the presence of a supervisor

Stay visible and match the energy of your floor.

A supervisor should always be visible or at least findable when needed. You should not appear to be relaxed when your staff is working hard, and you should show extreme interest in what your team is doing. It would be best if you indicated that you are following the flow step-by-step and that you are at the same wavelength and mentally updated and prepared for any situation, just like your team.

When you match the floor's speed, the employees feel that you are a team member; conversely, you are indirectly disrespecting their efforts in many ways when you are too relaxed. They will feel free to disrespect you in return whenever they feel like and not do what you ask. They can simply say: "It is easy to give orders; you are doing nothing."

Update and re-assess the situation.

A good supervisor keeps a timeline of "what is happening" for every stage throughout her shift. You have to hold an updated "Mental image" of the site in case of sudden changes. You should be able to summarize and review the situation in case of emergencies.

There will be sudden decisions to take and urgent questions from your boss to answer more often than you think. There will be a tired/sick employee who may decide to leave the shift in a crucial position halfway. *Do you have a replacement?* There may be a broken machine, and then you have to move your staff to another one. *Do you know which one is available?* If you do not prepare in advance and if you are too relax, and if you are not anticipating any troubles ahead of time, well, it is not good. You will enormously waste time and undoubtedly leaves your boss, "fuming."

Practical engagement.

Tour your work floor, come as close as possible safely near your staff, spend a few seconds looking at what they are doing, and leave agreeably; never mind murmurs or negative grimaces. Be there and let them get used to that. Let them feel your presence.

Do not forget that respect means taking someone into considerations whether he or she is present or not. Let them feel your presence and anticipate it when you are not there. You are not seeking your employee's approval when you are doing your job; emotions of discontent will regularly blow your way. If you feel the pressure in return because you do not like to be negative, try to have "thicker" skin, and grow up.

Your approach

If you are either too nice or too hard, that is not too good for this job. A good supervisor should never get involved emotionally with his daily transactions and ordeals. Too nice or too hard does not make professional personnel. Being involved emotionally with anything you do will affect your well-being, your performance, and your career's endurance in the long run.

The aggressive approach!

If you start off being pushy, it will undoubtedly lead you nowhere. It may get the job done for a while, only in your presence anyway, but it will make only the weaker employees work for you out of fear and eventually leave sick or depressed or even injured on purpose to avoid coming to work and still get paid.

Furthermore, you may have the genuine, hard-working employees very frustrated and subconsciously conspiring secretly on "not" doing the job next time when you are aggressive. They may start influencing others to do the same as they begin to build a support group against your negative approach.

With this approach, you will eventually lose your best troops to frustration and depression. Being aggressive will not work on your more hardy employees either, as it sets an instant resistance to you and a clash with their egos, which should be dealt with differently.

Some new supervisors use the «aggressive approach" to compensate for the lack of knowledge, but the smart employees will see through that. Many employees would sense that you are transmitting a weak emotion in being aggressive.

They will interpret your aggression for vulnerability and feel that you are yelling because you have to force your demands as if you are saying that "I am threatening you; if you do not do it, there will be consequences." Many people will frequently give you the opposite of what you want when you challenge them negatively.

In the long run, being aggressive will destroy the bridges of communication and trust between you and your staff, and it will hurt the company.

The Passive approach!

On the other hand, passivity does not go hand in hand with respect.

The too nice and too soft approach has the same effect as the aggressive one; you are transmitting a weak signal saying that "I am overwhelmed by the task of a supervisor, so I have to beg or bribe my way around."

The "too friendly" approach might work if your staff is in a good mood, and subsequently, your workers' response is out of pity, not out of respect. You do not want this kind of response. It automatically strips you of any authority you might have had, preventing you from being taken seriously, and ultimately, not deserving the "Leader" title.

As I put it previously, you can be yourself, and you can be empathetic when it comes to specific situations, but you have to establish your strong character first.

Your reputation must be: reliable and fair and "by the book" first, and THEN, and only then, you can reasonably respond to situations nicely if you want.

Establish your reputation while on probation.

If you are still on probation, YOU HAVE TO BE SOLID, NEVER FOLD, AND BY THE BOOK.

Do not change this approach until your probation period is over. For most companies, the probationary period is the first 3 to 6 months, where they put the new supervisor on examination and under observation. If, after that period, your scorecard is low, the job is on the line.

Most of the time, management listens to employees when they complain about your ways. And many employees love to volunteer and give you a low score at the tiniest mistake and report that to your boss. Instead, let your boss hear that you are serious, professional; let your boss get some complaints about you "not" handing out favors and that you are "not" too friendly, but do not let your boss hear that you are disrespectful to your employees also. You have to be assertive.

Being Assertive!!

Being Assertive is the way to go, and it means that you are doing your job without any charge from your emotions, and you are always in control.

The assertive person is always respectful to himself, the situation, and to everyone else. The "confident" person does not have to raise his voice; he is usually calm, and he reflects the general mood of the present situation. When it is urgent, he does not overreact, and he is always giving the right dose of attention and thought to every situation.

Your staff will like you and respect you for that; they will trust you and give you the lead; they will be happy to work for you, as they feel that they are in safe hands.

An assertive supervisor demonstrates to everyone that he does not fall for foolish games. Not bothered by jokes, and he does not have to respond to every silly comment and awkward question, and most importantly, is not easily provoked.

Your staff will stop wasting your time and the company's time. They will sense that their little mental games are not getting on your nerves and that you calmly and bravely are calling them on their stupidity at any time of the day.

The assertive supervisor:
• Knows how to say "No" without guilt.

- She does not justify a discipline if needed.
- He keeps his word and does not over-promise.

The assertive supervisor can say "yes or no," without any particle of guilt. All of her decisions are based on safety first, then on the company's benefit and its clients. In the long run, as it becomes your career, what do you say "yes or no" to, will define what kind of a supervisor you become.

Let me play out a common scenario: A supervisor who just started working in a company has decided that he would instead choose to be "understanding" to the employees' personal needs rather than following the company's policies. In this relatively short-staffed company, there is a strict policy on the "time of the year" when employees can go on vacation. However, everyone likes to go on vacation in July, and if many are given a holiday at the same time, you will end up with no one working for you that month. This situation will result in either the company goes extremely low on productions or hires and trains new staff members for only one month. Very very costly.

Nevertheless, to this new supervisor, all the excuses and arguments he heard like: "My wife takes her vacation in July, so I want July"; "My kids are off school in July, I cannot travel with them in March, can I?"; "I promised my dad to take him on a fishing trip in July, September is too cold for him.

All of that sounded like decent excuses to break the company's policy. So what do YOU do?

An assertive supervisor will undoubtedly consider and feel with most of the arguments but only apply what he find best for the company; he will feel no guilt in giving July only to who merits it and only according to the company rules and nothing else. Furthermore, an excellent assertive supervisor will gladly and calmly explain to the rest: why he did not grant their demands.

However, instead, if you give more vacation than you should, the management will step in either by breaking your word, cancel their holidays to save their business, or "break you" altogether and demote you and make you pay for the lost business. In both cases, you lose.

Minimum Absenteeism.

Everyone notices a supervisor's absence, not only when you are the direct boss for that department but also when you supervise other departments. Usually, employees take a mental count of who is present and who is absent. They ask questions such as: Is he fired? Is she sick? Are they together on vacation? And so on. Employees are so interested in the group of supervisors that lead their lives for hours and years. Everyone duly notes your absence in a big way.

A department without a supervisor is like a classroom without a teacher; it becomes messy and "free for all." However, in corporations, management is forced to find a substitution for any absent supervisor for the time being. It is not something they like to do without being notified in advance.

Moreover, when you become a frequent absentee yourself, it becomes challenging to discipline others for the same reason. You become exposed, and you lose a lot from your already-shaky integrity and respect.

Additionally, you may not last long in your position when you become a frequent abuser of the system yourself.

Dress the part.

In most companies, the supervisor has a distinctive costume from everyone else, and the reason is "The distinction" itself.
This difference is by design, and it is for you to be readily visible and be referred to if anything happens. It would be best to take care of your costume and keep in good condition, as it will serve you.

This costume will make you look a rank higher than your clerks, and it will grant you authority and weight, just like police, judges, or referees.

Just keep it tidy and clean; this way, you are more approachable; more likable, and look like a well-organized individual.

How does the assertive supervisor start the day?

Send a Clear Message every day.

The assertive supervisor starts the day with a clear, unmistakable message. This daily message is the pillar of your job; it is the "reminder" of who the boss is and how things will be from this moment onwards.

This message is the official start of the race; it is when the group's thoughts and muscles aim at the same objective.

Your "message" should be clear, organized, and delivered in a way that is understood. You should convey your message with clarity and directness. The way it is said, your voice tone and your posture should hold some hidden and unspoken messages, which will enforce your leadership: Ex:

-If you are new or they are a new group:

Present yourself, say your name with a clear voice, and talk briefly about your history in the company or outside.

-If you are not new:

Thank them for yesterday, say the results, and be precise:

"Thank you for yesterday, and because of you, the productivity was such-and-such." If productivity was low, say it, then say: "Today, I am expecting you to do better."

...And Talk about today's issues:

Say what you have, and say what your expectations are.

Stating your expectations is an essential part of your speech; say it clearly and repeat it if you have to. If you face resistance, repeat it loud and clear, do not forget; this is why you and everyone else is there. If people want to say something while you are talking, insist on finishing what you have to say first, and THEN you can take questions; if not, you will lose the train of thought, and you will never finish.

However, it would be best to balance talking and listening, but only after advancing your "daily" objectives first, then you can have a two-way dialogue.

After delivering your important message, let them speak, encourage them to ask if they have anything to say. When employees feel free to express their opinion about work, they tend to be more motivated and take more initiatives to prove their ideas.

Nevertheless, you should know the difference between constructive critique and valid questions from a waste-of-time. After listening for a couple of minutes, Feel free to stop the questions because they could be potent time wasters. When there are too many questions, you can respond by saying: "Please, enough for today, let us start working, if you have anything to say, I will see you during the day. I will pass by your stations".

Your personality!

The way you say your words and your general attitude enforce your character as a respectable person. Your unspoken communication, while delivering your message, should hold these hidden suggestions:

• I am talking to you with full confidence.

• I may raise my voice because I want the message to be very clear.

• I do not want to repeat myself, and I know that you will do your job because it is your job. I am not asking.

• I do not care for those of you who are talking and laughing, and I have no time to respond, but you will be accountable if I said something now, and you ignored it or forgot about it later.

Find your way, your own culture; find what is acceptable in your environment; I cannot tell you what to say word-for-word; every day is different, and so is every company and supervisor. The voice tone, facial expression, and body language play a crucial role in showing your assertiveness; it is something you can practice and eventually master.

Practice Public speaking!

The speech is the mirror of the soul; you are what you say, and more important is how you say it.

As a supervisor, you will hold many meetings, including group meetings, one-on-one meetings, and meetings with your boss and your union representatives.

Speaking is your weapon since, in many companies, a supervisor does not work with his hands.

You need to sharpen your "Public Speaking" skills to communicate what you want.

The most crucial communication element is clarity, and a clear idea consists of organized thoughts, a clear voice tone, and good delivery.

When you talk to one person or a group of people, your effectiveness depends on how straightforward your message is and whether your words are in the right context—one of the fundamental reasons for disagreement is: words misunderstood and intentions unclear. Therefore, be clear, state what you want, and don't "beat around the bush."

Gibran Khalil Gibran once said, "Between what is said and not meant, and what is meant and not said, most of the love is lost."

I would suggest that you go for some proper training on the art of public speaking, and if you cannot, go through some "personal" practices, as simple as talking to yourself in the mirror. Listen to yourself talk, record yourself, and ask a good friend for his opinion.

The "art of public speaking" will enable you to speak with precision and use fewer words, as you would know precisely what you ought to say. Another beneficial effect is that you would hold subordinates accountable for undone jobs or poorly done assignments because you were undoubtedly clear when giving them instructions about tasks to be carried out.

Deliver your words with convictions

Experience and repetition will give you the power to say what you want without any hesitation and with visible conviction.
This ability to deliver your speech with conviction is the secret to self-confidence on the job. Know what you are talking about and believe in it. Study your work if you have to, and with time, you will master it, the same way you have learned your old job.

Before attending meetings, practice what you would say.

Before a meeting for any critical issue, write down what you say on a piece of paper, formulate your questions, and highlight the strong headlines. After that, and on your own, practice it, repeat it until you become an expert, fluent.

Go further and prepare possible counter-arguments and prepare your response to the response. In short, be more than prepared. For discipline meetings, or any meeting should not leave you stuttering!

For you, this might be just another meeting, but it is of utmost importance for the people you supervise, such as if their careers are on the line.

A supervisor leading the way.

You are the boss, so your speech should exude confidence, however, with an appropriate amount of respect for the people you would be presiding over. In your addresses, let there be clear deadlines and ultimatums, which you must follow as well, and treat your words with weightiness. If you have to warn an employee, ensure you have the appropriate body language that comes with such a talk. Move close to the employee, use their names, make eye contact, and make your message short and definite. Sound dead serious. No, this does not mean you should sound threatening, but you should communicate very seriously and professionally. The way you handle such a scenario could prevent you from having hassles with the rest of them later on, and it creates a mark of what you represent in their minds.

The way you keep your staff informed.

The supervisor is the link between the management and the workers. He is the messenger, and he is the executor.

Sometimes you are the good news bearer, but you are the bad news bearer most of the time. When it comes to slashing positions, it is for you to announce, and when the management decides to speed up the process to increase productivity, you are giving the news and enforcing the new norms.

The way you inform your staff is very crucial in implementing and respecting the new demands. A good supervisor always transmits the new norms as-a-matter-of-fact; he is not justifying, and mostly he is not feeling guilty about it.

Never deflect the responsibility, and do not divert blame onto others. "They told me to say so," or "It is their decision" are phrases that weaken your connection and your representation of your company and thus underestimate your powers. Say it as if it is your decision too. Try to prepare valid "business-related" justifications for the new rules, even if your management did not give you any. You should right away adapt the new decisions as your own.

Leading and transferring some of the responsibility.

Every day, your staff complete the work assigned for that day, but from time to time, you may wish that you can personally intervene and manually help or speed up a situation because the job is incomplete. But the time is almost up, and you cannot.

Instead, it would be best to foresee the delay and delegate significant responsibilities ahead of time to your staff. You can do that by holding your team fully accountable for the lack of it. Proactively, you should ensure that everyone, you and they, feel the same sense of urgency and predict the lateness.

You can transmit the sentiment by first: giving them enough support and trust. Second: by a clear message of the target to be achieved safely and efficiently, and then: by registering in their minds the "responsibility, accountability and consequences" trio.

In the last chapter of this book, you will have a lot of advice in dealing with your staff.

CHAPTER 2

HOW TO RELATE WITH YOUR BOSS

COMPANY LADDER

By working faithfully eight hours a day, you may eventually get to be "Boss" and work twelve hours a day.

Robert Frost

The boss-subordinate relationship is not one which you choose; it is imposed upon you. Your personalities might clash, and you may see things from different perspectives, but the most important thing to remember is that your boss is your boss!

The relation with your boss!

You don't have to like him or her; you only have to accept that they are your boss. Liking or disliking your boss should never be an issue.

I once asked a manager about his director, "Do you like your boss? He said, I don't have to like him, I work for him, yes he is tough, but I would be the same if I were in his shoes. I fancied that answer because it was a logical answer given by someone who'd chosen not to mix up professional and personal issues. That manager also proved that he didn't need any emotional approval (Positive or negative) to go on with his day, and in fact, why should you? After all, your boss is not your friend, and this relationship is strictly on professional grounds. Your boss to you: is like you to your employees.

A smart manager will never dis-like her supervisors as some people claim for no justifiable reason; your boss depends solely on you to look good in front of her boss. A lousy manager might blame you for failure in some cases, but her boss will not tolerate her criticism of you for long. Big bosses want only results.

In normal circumstances, you should see yourself as "the sum of your employees" to your boss. A supervisor (you) depends on 25 people to look good in front of his boss. A manager (your boss) depends on one or two to do the same.

He wants a good relationship with you. So don't feel alienated by him, because even if it does feel like it, managers have nothing to gain from making your life miserable, except for the rare exception.

Remember, more responsibility is placed on his shoulders if things go south from your side.

Learning by taking notes!

As a rule, when you are in a new position, they will teach you what to do. Management may give you a couple of weeks' course and give you a few days to shadow someone and learn as you go. Take notes, and write everything down. Don't assume you'll remember everything; you can't- so please take notes!

Until they give you the green light that you are ready to go on your own, keep taking notes and keep organizing it, you will unmistakably use it later.

When I started in my new position as a supervisor, my notes on any given day were transferred and filtered after work at home and placed in a select file. And by doing that after work, I was not working for "them" for free; I was working for me; I reinforced the knowledge I would use for years to come.

A wise man once said, "Wise people learn when they can, fools learn when they must," so learn your job while you can, do it for yourself. You will work better, look better, and ultimately feel better.

You studied for free at home when you went to school to improve yourself, and you have looked for a day like today— a day where you have a good job that you want to maintain. And to learn now for your new job, a few hours at the onset of a new career is more rewarding financially and personally than you'll ever think.

By taking notes publicly in your workplace, you will leave a great impression on your boss and management as a whole. It shows your willingness, it shows your engagement, and besides, they won't have to explain the same thing multiple times for you to catch on. It will also show that if you answer any question in the future, you're not just saying anything; you have it all written down. Imagine if you had to say the same thing over and over again to an employee, wouldn't you feel somewhat cranky? Exactly, you don't want your boss to feel this way about you!

After several years of experience, I was still taking occasional notes here and there; notes on some long sequence to remember and notes on a particular operation step-by-step that I may forget otherwise.

When your boss gives you a directive or a procedure to follow, you should keep the practice of writing what he wants. This good habit will serve two purposes:

1- The obvious, it will make you remember details of what he said.

2- It will serve as proof of blamelessness in case "he" made a mistake. For instance: I told you Monday, not Tuesday. No sir. You said Tuesday; here the proof. Again, with a simple act of taking notes, you are putting less strain on your brain and eliminating the possibility of forgetfulness after a full and busy day.

Daily and weekly reports!

Your reports have a timeline, and you have to send them to your boss at the exact time of the day, so don't wait for the last minute to do everything. The best strategy is to keep the report files handy, and whenever you can have a moment or two, update your files.

When you leave those reports till the last hour or the last day, I'll guarantee you that they'll come out poorly organized and with several loopholes; it'll look like a terrible copy-and-paste case, one which your boss can spot from a mile away.

I have witnessed a couple of supervisors getting in trouble because of the last-minute habit; it pushed them to falsify signatures while attempting to cover up for their laziness and lateness, and eventually, it got them fired.

A report that is updated daily is automatically rich and full, it comes out much better than a rushed job, and it comes without putting in much-concentrated effort into it. Sometimes "poco-a-poco" is the way to go!

Preparations for "self" evaluation

Your "self-evaluation" is the time when you're officially allowed to brag about yourself. So please do it. And do it with "vengeance." There is nothing wrong with that. They are paying for your services, so tell them what you have done for them lately.

It would help if you prepared your annual or semi-annual "evaluation" in advance. A director once told me that he has a PowerPoint file open for the year, and he doesn't wait until the last day to register his achievements. Every time he believes that he had accomplished something special, he would immediately update that file with pictures, details, and descriptions. He added that the file was always full and ready before time, and if he had never followed that method, 60% of his achievements would have gone unnoticed and forgotten.

So please keep track of your accomplishments, keep them handy; you never know.

"Preparation" is always right.

At the beginning of the coronavirus pandemic, my boss called me at home and asked me desperately if I know the staff's phone numbers over the age of 65 because we have to call them immediately and ask them to stay home. (Now that I'm not a supervisor anymore, but still preparing as a habit). It was a Sunday night, and the calls have to start quickly to prevent them from coming to work Monday morning and risk their lives.

My boss knows that for statistics reasons, I have everything. I only had to connect from home and get the info. While I was talking to him, he said: by the way, I have the company's vice-president on the line with us, and he's listening, and we appreciate you helping and taking the call at night.

Whether you prepare for your evaluation or anything work-related, this is a critical practice to maintain throughout your career. It would be best if you always did it when information is fresh in your head and while you still have access to it. Because when you leave that to the last day, you are likely to keep scratching your head and probably end up writing not-so-great flashes that are improperly captured.

Learn your boss's job and drive for results.

Your job is a part of your boss's business; you are a piece in the puzzle, so why not learn the whole thing? The big picture. By understanding her work, you're not only accumulating experience for further promotion, but you are also anticipating in advance what your boss's concerns are and what "stimulates" the movement in your company.

When you know what she is dealing with daily, you will automatically focus your efforts on things that you are more likely to be asked for instead of wasting your energy on irrelevant affairs. If you work in this way, you'd soon become an indispensable supervisor who is deeply admired by the boss, and who knows! You might get a recommendation for promotion. Although certainly, you are earning her respect.

Once in a while, good supervisors lose the compass and start to waste their focus on the wrong battles. They get hung on an idea or on something else that only makes sense to them. These supervisors' efforts usually go unnoticed and unappreciated. And then they start to grow impatient with their boss and the company itself, and they think: "I know that I'm putting the hours and the effort, why is it that there is no recognition nor any hints for promotion for me?"

Two things you should always keep in mind and evaluate periodically:

1- You should know that as much as you are encouraged to think outside the box, there is still the "company way," and your boss wants you to do just that.

2- You should always focus on results. Please don't waste your time making that sheet that will take hours to build when it's time for you to be with your staff enforcing productivity and safety. And please don't focus on an "already profitable" sector and neglect that "suffering" other.

Your boss wants nothing more than seeing that green, positive indicator on the result sheet to present it to her boss. You will earn her respect and support, and she will know that you are not diverting from the primary goal. The term "Driving for results" is more complicated than this but is also as simple as that.

Yes, I can!

A positive can-do attitude is a big booster to the relation with your boss. He will immediately open up to you, and he will start to share all of his concerns and ideas, and eventually, you become part of his plans. But most importantly, you become the number one contender for promotion, mostly if you rarely "complain" or seldom "decline."

When you always keep that openness mindset, you will become a significant influence for the other supervisors who now see as "the" good example. Your boss will gladly appreciate that positive influence that affects the team as a whole and puts you as their natural "next" leader.

Complex situations, emergencies!

Every job in any company has "regular" daily procedures, a plan, a to-do list of meetings, reports, observations, etc., of things to do, and a specific route from A to Z to sufficiently complete your day. These "regular" procedures are several ideas that were modified, adjusted, and updated throughout the years to have reached the way it is now. Most days, and by just following the "regular" procedures, it is enough for you to achieve your goals. <u>But a "complex" situation -like an emergency- can develop at any moment, disturb the daily procedures, and negatively influence the outcome.</u>

These situations separate men from boys; in other words, it's when your instinct, improvisation, and calmness control the problem and not the other way around.

Would you run to your boss?

Do you panic?

Or do you ignore it? And you wish it is the end of your shift?

Every situation has a different set of procedures but most importantly is you. You have <u>to stay calm,</u> but also you have to have a sense of urgency as well. You <u>should not panic</u> and lose control, but you <u>have to be strict</u> and direct your group to overcome the ordeal. It would be best if you only let your boss know the extreme situations and never run to him for every single incident.

Adapt for change.

Since the mid-1990s and computer technology and industrial machinery are progressing rapidly, no one can keep up. From software to hardware to any machine that can use a "motherboard," the updates are frequent, and the change is imminent. And for that, your company/factory hires new generations of engineers and technicians regularly to update machines and software for the latest technology. And if you are not ready to adapt as well, it will not be easy. You have to be open and not attached to old habits, and often you have to forget about a procedure you did for a long time and learn something new.

You have to keep your mind open, and your spirit, you shouldn't feel under stress when diverting from the routine. It is not a choice; because a time will come where you have to forget about the "facility" of doing your job on cruise-control after years of experience and get back to class to learn the ABCs of something new.

You have to forget about the old method because now, a 24 years old new engineer has convinced management of his "new" approach, and you are obliged to conform. You have to accept, and you have to adapt. The young engineer is most probably right.

Accept criticism from the boss.

Your boss is the best person qualified to give you the right criticism to excel in your job. He knows what you have and what you don't. Accept it, ask for it and read it from between the lines when he speaks to you. His criticism is usually direct and to the point. The criticism of a boss is mostly work-related, so don't take it personally. As much as everybody likes to avoid criticism and look good, you should seek his. Ask him questions a few weeks before your evaluation, "what can I work on?" and work on the points he gives you before he has to mention it officially and with consequences.

CHAPTER 3

HOW TO RELATE WITH OTHER SUPERVISORS

TEAMWORK

There are two kinds of people, those who do the work and those who take the credit. Try to be in the first group; there is less competition there.

Indira Gandhi

In most companies, you will find yourself working daily with a "team" of supervisors: a group with almost the same amount of responsibilities, tasks, and paperwork to complete.

From the employee's perspective, the supervisors represent the same thing. They think that if supervisors are always together, eating, talking, and socializing as a separate group, they are for sure conspiring also against the workers, " I feel like every supervisor is watching me." That's what one employee told me once. "You! supervisors- are a mafia; you all network and share info," he added. So by only a silhouette of any supervisor passing by, most clerks will adjust their postures and speed to look busy, regardless of who the supervisor is.

It is like when you see a police car, what readily comes to mind? It is highly unlikely that you pay much attention to the police officer in the car as an entity; you are more likely to think of what this person represents and care less about what they had for dinner last night! It's the uniform and what it means, and you understand that once you crossed that red light, regardless of who is in the trooper car, he or she will nail you. From the employee's point of view, no significant difference among supervisors exists. They are and behave as a unit.

The same consequences and rewards are expected by whoever is doing the job, so don't disappoint them.

From the supervisors' perspective, you will notice that every supervisor is different. Despite working in unison and under the same directions, everyone has different skill sets, characters, and attitudes towards work and life. They are like any other part of society: distinct individuals, and by all means.

In most cases, supervisors don't work as a unit; although they should, they are more likely to work independently or in pairs.

There are all kinds of supervisors (human beings) you will deal with daily, and you should prepare yourself.

So, how should you, as a new supervisor, identify and deal with each of the other supervisors? The good news is: most supervisors are good supervisors, and they are there to work and earn their living.

But every rule has some exceptions. Here are a couple of examples of different supervisors and how you might deal with them.

The Super-supervisor!

Everyone is carrying his baggage, background, education, and own different approach and life experience. Sometimes, you will work with that one supervisor who has more drive than anyone else and more motivated.

This person arrives earlier than everyone else, more prepared, more focused, and usually has an excellent work-related memory, and he can stay late.

Your first instinct is maybe feeling threatened by this individual, but you must resist that instinct; he is a good ally. Instead, work together, let him plow the road, ride his wave, befriend him. Propose to split the tasks and take note of his apparent strengths and learn from him. Don't try to bump into him or her; work synergistically, take on the other functions you see yourself better at performing and join troops with this tank.

This super-supervisor is naturally and effortlessly better than most, and It's so wrong to start comparing or even competing with him or her. He may represent a threat to the other supervisors, but not you; just be yourself and choose to work in synchrony.

The useless supervisor!

He is "the" always late, unprepared, and never up-to-date supervisor.

This person's typical answers are:

· Well, they didn't tell me.

· Oh, I wasn't here.

· No, I can't help you next Tuesday; I might take the day off.

· My car broke down.

This "dude" has somehow passed through the system and seems to be above the law to some extent.

Even though there are repeated complaints about him or her, there is nothing they can do.

The best way to deal with this supervisor is to stick to your tasks and not be bothered by his carelessness level. Anticipate what he will "miss" or "forget" and warn your boss indirectly. BUT don't work for the 2 of you, and stay aware that your boss will ask you to help him. Ask for extra time if you want to help him, but don't work on your time for both. It can become a habit of everyone.

The unconvinced supervisor!

A very challenging supervisor to work with is the supervisor who is on a constant mission to prove himself. Usually, he comes with low self-esteem and a bad temper, and the inevitable daily encounters with the boss for a minute-by-minute support session. He likes to showcase his achievements and snitch on his friends. Subsequently, this mindset makes him an informant, a back-stabber, and always taking the credit when the team accomplishes a task.

With this type, prepare to stay calm about your feelings and sentiments towards the company and the boss. Don't discuss with him your daily mishaps and mistakes.

Don't whine about other supervisors or even employees. He will use it against you when he needs it. He continuously believes that it is not enough and that he is an underachiever in his head.

Despite his faulty attributes, this supervisor type is generally a good worker. A kind compliment naturally raises his morale, and a simple thumbs-up will make him feel good. Compliment his work from time to time, and you can depend on his collaboration at all times.

The arrogant supervisor!!

The other bad example of a supervisor would be the prominent arrogant and selfish supervisor. He can sometimes be disrespectful and full of himself. So watch out. Avoid them, but don't refuse to work with him if they ask you to do it. It's your job. You can do nothing about this one; do your job and don't seek his or her support. They can be bossy and controlling, don't play their game. Stay genuinely busy and don't open up to them just to pass the time.

The BIG question

As a supervisor, how should you behave with all the different types, bad and good? Is there a "one way" to deal with all supervisors? The answer is: yes, but start with *yourself.*

Dealing with self-doubt <u>first.</u>

You have to know that they chose you and saw you fit and then have trained you for this job, so you should stop worrying and always be eager to prove yourself. Despite having some difficult days, it doesn't mean that your job is on the line after every incident. Relax. You will have some difficult situations, and you will have nights where it seems like it is not ok, but that is the job, and that is the atmosphere you will be in for quite some time.

Eventually, the same atmosphere stays, but your feelings towards it change. You will get used to it. And you will be enjoying it and performing it at the highest level.

Go easy on yourself.

More than you think, many new supervisors involuntarily pushed themselves off the cliff by quitting their jobs prematurely. They couldn't take the pressure anymore, so they end their careers precipitately by leaving under stress. Too much stress can make you lose it. Many anticipate the terrible results from their boss, which is maybe not true, so they quit in advance. Please, don't do that. You may be wrong. And even if you get fired, face it, and ask for the reasons. Fight it or learn from it.

To avoid going down this path:

1.   Act logically at all times.

2.   Remove your "personality" from the mix; it's not personal.

3.   Remember that they hire you because they want you as you are.

4.   Remind yourself that you are excellent, and you can make the right judgment calls.

5.   Keep your mind free from worries.

6.   Most supervisors are going through the same ups-and-downs; you don't see them because they act nonchalant.

7.   You are doing the same things day in day out. Eventually, it will become second nature.

8.   If he can do it and she can do it, I for sure can.

Dealing with situations

Deal with every situation reasonably and urgently, instead of dealing with them nervously or desperately. The "always worried and always desperate attitude" can badly affect your judgment, and it will make you do bad calls and eventually fail miserably in what you do.

Dealing with all supervisors.

Generally speaking, when dealing with your colleagues, the most important thing is identifying them; you should recognize what kind of supervisors they are.

And you should be ready with the right "attitude/response," prepared for every one of them.

As a rule, you should treat everyone with respect, along with staying alert. It should take a couple of weeks to identify their behaviors and take mental notes of them. Remember, the majority are regular people like you, and they are there to work and help others; you can relax.

In contrast, start to identify those special characters we spoke about before. After identifying and labeling them:

- Get ready.
- Make sure you adjust your personality accordingly.
- Gently let them know that you wouldn't be carrying out any tasks that aren't clearly stated in your job description.
- Don't try to impress anyone.
- Don't seek approval from other supervisors; no one cares except your boss.
- Reconsider your opinion about who you thought is "bad" or "good" regularly; many take time for you to recognize.
- Be firm and make your stance clear without being rude; refuse to be used!
- When you have been paired to carry out the same task for that day, make sure that duties are divided evenly among you.

Show some adaptability!

You can agreeably choose to split the tasks as everyone is better at different things: Volunteer to do the reports if you are a faster "type" while the other is a better communicator with the staff or vice versa.

If you are working with a fair and just supervisor, great, that can be a bonus, but always be prepared to handle the hostile ones.

When dealing with a "too nice" no leadership kind of a person, there could be some advantages, but it also comes with its peculiarities. It will be satisfying on your morale, and you'll feel respected, but physically and mentally, it could be a little demanding because you are thinking for 2.

Always think first; always assess the new situation or the new partner or the new task. Be realistic, and let go of the desire to have ready-made or pre-assembled solutions.

Instead, be ready to craft out unconventional solutions as the case demands of you. Don't wish for things to fall from the sky and assemble themselves. You can be spontaneous and natural with friends and family, but at work, pause and reflect; others are planning, and they are now a few steps ahead of you.

It's also crucial that you do not run directly to your boss whenever a misunderstanding occurs between you and another supervisor.

Your boss should only know about work-related issues; strike out the need to have your boss interfere in character-related matters. Especially sensitive topics and the "he said, she said" kind of problems; your boss should not be bothered by it.

Share personal experiences and strength!

You can benefit others and yourself when you actively share what you know. You and everyone else poses a unique talent of some sort; don't hide it. If this talent helps in your field, you will be doing everyone a favor when you share. You can almost always show a new or an old supervisor a piece of technical advice or a mathematical trick that would make the job easier. Your relation with your peers would take a different direction when you initiate generosity in showing a new trade trick.

The return of this generosity will have many forms:

- Many will teach you something in return.
- Most will be extra friendly just for your gesture.
- Few will be eager to pay you back with work and nonwork-related compensation.
- Your boss will see it.

Be aware of the supervisor training you.

Sometimes that person can make a slave of you for generations to come. But not always, only when you let it happen.

Last word

Most supervisors are like you. They want to be good at their job and earn respect. Eventually, they will professionally and personally conform to the company's norms and behave alike and support each other. You will earn their respect and establish your reputation by being strong, proactive, and organized.

CHAPTER 4

DOS AND DON'TS

TO ELIMINATE STRESS

> *When you are content to be yourself*
> *and don't compete and compare,*
> *everybody will respect you and live*
> *stress-free.*
>
> *Chinese proverb*

A bunch of good habits makes a successful person excel at what he or she is doing. Here, you will have a collection of "Do's and Don'ts" that I hope you can refer to; a simple job-aide to eliminate the stress and earn the respect you deserve.

TO ELIMINATE STRESS

Going early to work —

A good supervisor is rarely late, and most of the time is there before anyone else. You have to be there early enough to assess the situation before operations start and be surprised. A mental picture of the day's tasks before anyone comes to work is very crucial. You don't have to be there hours before; 45 minutes are perfect for preparing for an eight-hour shift. Why is it essential?

• By coming early and preparing for the day, you are taking a mental snapshot of your battlefield before strategically placing your soldiers in their designated positions.

• It will allow quick choices and an early start to your operations without wasting valuable minutes on decisions.

• You are eliminating surprises, and by doing that, you are minimizing the chance of any hassle that would raise your stress level later and make you forget essential things.

• It will show your boss: your dedication, and you will become a promotion material.

Honestly, keep it between us; when you come to work 30 to 45 minutes before your shift starts, you can have a couple of hours of relaxation— cruising on low gear during your shift.

Be Prepared!

As a supervisor, there is nothing better than proper preparation. It seems foolhardy that any supervisor wouldn't deem it necessary to be well-prepared for the day's tasks. A good habit of preparing in advance keeps you updated, confident, and calm.

Don't Leave your reports and work for the last minute. When you leave assignments for the last minute, you will feel stressed because you'll keep ruminating upon it and thinking of the consequences resulting from if you can't make it on time. And when you finally make it rush-rush, your work will be incomplete and full of errors. It's an unwanted awful feeling that makes some people hate their job.

Learning.

Everyone knows the importance of learning new things. But when the daily cycle overwhelms you, it feels like there is barely enough time to finish what you have on hands.

Try to dedicate an hour a day to learn a new subject or, even better, a work-related topic that may deepen your knowledge in what you do.

Learning is an excellent motivator for becoming successful and one of the most valid indications to you and others (your boss) that you WANT to advance in your career and life. Again, the wise man says, "The wise learn when he can, and the fool learns when he must." By learning and accumulating knowledge about your domain, you solve problems before they even appear and eliminate stress from your life.

Besides, When you are more technically advanced, your days are more pleasant, and you perform tasks with utmost finesse and speed; if a job used to take two hours to complete, now you do it perfectly well within 30 minutes!.

Moreover, when you have skills in your work-related industry, your boss would take you off the "battlefield" and put you on more meaningful projects. In other words, you will rapidly gain the confidence of your boss, and he or she replaces your work on the battleground with a calmer and more productive one in the planning office.

Don't over-promise!

When you promise, you should follow through. Yes, a promise is not a legal obligation, nor is it a contract.

Still, it has more considerable gravitation and more consequences than promising your friends, when you are at work or in any professional setting.

At work, a promise puts you in a stressful mental state as this promise is on "standby" in your head, and it may hinder the work effort from others towards you because they are expecting something from you first.

You should only promise what you can follow through, and don't just promise anything to lubricate a "tight" situation with future false hopes. Eventually, overpromising will diminish your credibility and respect and strips your word from any weight.

Don't be a control freak.

A control freak is a micromanager who likes to attend to every single case and detail. This person would manipulate others and put pressure to get the results he wants. This approach is very stressful for both you and others when you become the controller. A control freak is untrusting by nature and believes that only his way will achieve these results.

He becomes obsessed with people doing it—the way he told them to do it. And in return, and because he doesn't respect the different approaches that others take, they make sure his system fails.

The employees indirectly wish to prove him wrong all the time—sometimes subconsciously and other times, well...consciously!.

Furthermore, a control freak looks at every detail, which will drain him and make him forget about the big picture entirely. Micromanaging takes up all of your time because you are managing everything, or at least, that's what you think. Instead, let nature and time and the excellence in others pave your way, trust, and establish a good relationship with them, and then sit down and enjoy the view.

Delegate!!

The natural response to micromanaging is to become a supervisor who knows how to delegate and move on.

A good supervisor can easily delegate what she wants with the appropriate authority and responsibility given to her employees.

- She knows her expectations and anticipates results.
- She doesn't need permission to ask for what she wants.
- She is clear and encouraging, and she makes them want to show her that they are also capable of excellence.

Furthermore, any employee can look busy for 8 hours without having to do one productive task. Feel free to stop them from whatever they are doing, and tell them what you want. Ask for volunteers initially or ask anyone to "prove" his alternatives if he suggests any. If none, tell them what you want.

To sum up, the delegation approach is: asking for it directly; without any hesitation or apologies, it's your job.

Don't overreact!!

People sometimes like to give importance to what they do, and they do it by overreacting to minor situations. They easily verbalize "frustration" and "how difficult their day is"; don't be like this. This type of "reaction" to every situation multiplies your stress level and label you as "panicky" and unreliable.

As a supervisor, you will have a daily occurrence with small hassles. Don't make it worse than it is. Relax, assess the problem, look for solutions, or ask your boss. Don't overreact to things that will reoccur regularly, especially if they aren't vital.

Let your employees show you their strengths.

This one is good for both stress management and respect. Most people tend to possess some fields of superiority, so let them shine.

Ask their opinions on specific issues that you know they are good at. Don't cut their wings by being a bossy boss, a micro boss. Let them be, let them improvise, and think outside the box. Maybe they have a better idea; if someone suggests something, tell this employee: prove it, do it. I'm behind you. Your staff will feel good about themselves and excel on their own.

Can't change everything!!

The company, the human nature, and bureaucracies were here before you and will continue after you. Please give it up; you can't change much.

Yes, you might have a vision and a different approach, but when this approach is consuming you mentally or professionally, give it up. Address the issues and not the people; try to solve your problems by changing some small cases one at a time and not changing the big picture. The best "change" is the one that begins from within.

TO EARN THE RESPECT

Accept criticism and apologize if wrong.

Life is not a "popularity" contest unless you're still "maturely" in high school. Accept criticism with an open mind. Own a thick skin. Many people will not be diplomatic in criticizing you, but so what? You will always learn something from every critic regardless of how unfounded or unfair the criticism is.

Listen to what people say; even jokes have some reality. When your employees or your boss say something, read between the lines, listen. When you accept the criticism, you define your character in their eyes as fearless of criticism and not bothered about being wrong. And when you're wrong, apologize because you demand them to do so. Take responsibility, and it will raise your points.

Be self-aware!

Most people are not aware of their impact on others. And in our case, the supervisor-employee relationship is very delicate. So you should know that:

- As the supervisor, you are an automatic "alpha," and you should be the dominant figure in the workplace among the 2, so less is more.

- You don't have to say much, and you don't have to abuse.

- A simple remark from you has an impact. You don't have to scream.

- Don't repeat yourself too much, and don't take yourself lightly; in the same token, respect yourself and don't fool around jokingly.

- Respect your employees and talk to them in the tone you want them to talk back to you.

As I said before, glimpsing anything that may look like the supervisor's "shirt color" passing by will make a slacking worker—work.

Self-perception is relative to the situation in front of us. Most of the time, we overreact or underestimate or even destroy the "good image" we once had just to prove a stupid point, and is it worth it?

The best strategy to become self-aware is to have an exemplary character or a personality you look up to and try to compare-to; "if this person was here instead of me, how would he or she have reacted to the situation"? Then act likewise, with calmness and composure!

NOT too much empathy!

Empathy is a civilized and humane virtue, and not too many people have it, but as a supervisor and a decision-maker, holding on to it is counterproductive. You are dealing with humans, but you can't forgive every situation because it is difficult and because you feel the other person's pain.

Success is achieved with sweat and tears; money and lives earned dearly. And as a boss, you will have many subordinates try to play on your emotions, and by showing too much empathy, they will "take you for a ride" every day, and employees will perceive you as "soft."

If you put yourself in their place and sympathize with every "I have a headache" excuse and every "I feel tired" justification or every "I'm a single parent" plea, you will not get anything done. Your boss will still ask you for the results, and he will not accept the lack of productivity. You are paid for that, and so are your employees.

Stick to your word, and be careful what you say!

Sticking to your word and keeping your promise is who you are, and it is the essence of respect.

Your relation with your employees is based on civilized communication and mutual respect.

Your "speech" is what motivates them. Your word is what "assure" them and what "make" or "break" them. Your employees are not chained to their workstations, nor are you whipping them to advance; your employees relate to you and the job by what you tell them to do and how you say it, and of course, by the salary every two weeks.

And "what you tell them" is very important in maintaining the workflow and your respect. So try to keep your words:

- Work-related
- To the point
- Minimum jokes
- No flip-flop
- Clear
- When you say something, please do it.
- Don't mention ultimatums if you are not going to keep.

Remember, the employees listen when the supervisor talks; it is the "call of duty," which could be the source of stress or relief. So be careful and chose your words wisely and the tone it is said. The comments from a supervisor carry weight, and it has an impact. So keep it meaningful. The effect of your right words gives them security, a feeling of justice, and respect.

When they know that everything you've promised and every request or deadline you've announced will undoubtedly come true—contrary to what you thought—they will feel good.

It will give your employees the safety and guidance of a "shepherd" taking care of business for them and guaranteeing the continuity of their careers and success.

Employees might complain about a demanding supervisor, but they favor him over a weak one.

Be "friendly," but not "friends."

To earn someone's respect, you have to respect them first. Your employees are looking at you all the time, listening to what you say and how you say it. Your team, just like little kids, are subconsciously seeking your approval and gratitude and working on being friendly with you. They hope that this can promote their relationship with you to a "friend" category that will facilitate life with you. So beware, you can be "friendly" but not friends. Seeking your friendship is a natural and a positive connection, but your employees seek it for the wrong reasons.

You should always maintain a keen sense of professionalism with your staff because once you cross that line, it becomes difficult to properly and seriously discipline a "friend." And for some people, once they cross the psychological barrier with you, they feel less pressured at work, and they will "take it easy."

You have to find the fine line between friendly and friends; if not, you are automatically eliminating your power to make decisions and to show that you are in control.

Think about your friends; how easy is it to coach them, manage them, or give them directions? Not likely to be very easy! So, don't make the job of a supervisor more challenging for yourself.

Don't conspire against your boss or the company.

Many new supervisors start to badmouth their bosses and the company decisions to win their staff's cooperation and approval. They begin to deflect the blame onto their bosses, especially if there are any new strict measures taken, to withdraw themselves from the confrontations. "I don't agree, but they told me to say so." "I wanted to give you the day off, but my manager said no."

Instead of taking the company's side with any conflict, those supervisors criticize the company secretly and take the employees' side.

By doing so, the supervisor will not get any "points" nor the desired cooperation from his employees; instead, by disrespecting the company and his boss, whom he represents: he is underestimating his moral worth by betraying "who he represents."

But the most damaging effect of such behavior is that: this supervisor now gave the employees the freedom and the "guts" and the "carte blanche" to criticize any new work order, any change, or any new rule he wants to implement. Now, he opened the door for his employees to reject any new work order and refrain from doing it. "Another stupid law." "They don't know what they are doing as usual." "You do agree, right!! This is not good, I'm not doing it." and the worst is when your employee tells you: " Go get me your boss, I want to talk to him."

You are the company, and the company is you. But now you became nobody; you became a walking shadow. Take the side of the company; you are part of management.

How to apply discipline respectfully?!

In a unionized or non-unionized company, applying discipline must follow a set of written or unwritten rules to win your case when it comes to arbitration.

Before disciplining, you have to make sure that:

• You warned the employee one last time before the discipline.

• You explained the consequences of replicating the "disputed" behavior.

• You followed the legitimate steps in your company.

• Despite the conflict, you maintained a respectful tone.

- You didn't show grudges afterward.
- You are addressing the issue and not the person.

The next day, you proceed as if nothing has happened; you were only doing your job. You stay professional and very respectful.

Follow on your employee's requests.

You expect them to do what you ask, so please do what they ask you to do. Most of the time, these requests are about salary, vacation time, or medical reports. These issues might not be "significant" for you, but it is essential for them. Especially anything related to their salary; it's their livelihood, and it's why they are here in the first place.

Your employees expect you to attend to their needs because you are the first liaison between them and the company. And most importantly, you don't want to have a worried employee working; he or she will not be at their peak of productivity in an anxious, tense state. And finally, helping them when they need you displays a good deal of mutual respect.

Know when and where to draw the line!

The bigger the group of employees, the more boundaries you need to impose, or you will definitely lose control.

In some cases, you have to say NO to a "simple request," not because you are a "difficult" supervisor, but because if you say YES, then "the simple request" becomes a complicated one.

Ex1: If you say YES to a day-off requested by an employee for "tomorrow" in the middle of a busy week because he feels tired, you will instantly come to realize that your employees communicate with each other at the speed of light. Because by the time the employee returns to his station, 7 or 8 employees already heard about the favor he got. And I guarantee you that half of them will no doubt ask you for the same day. And by being fair and just, you say YES to all; and you end-up with a short-staffed day. And good luck explaining that to your boss. Instead, anticipate, and think not with your heart.

Ex2: During meetings, you know that the same employees ask for permission to speak, and you also know that they want to protest something or show discontent or complain about something you've heard before. Every day the same group is wasting valuable time from you and the company. You heard them tens of times, and it is always the same issue.

Here you must "draw the line" and say enough is enough; in many cases, issues have been raised on purpose, either to waste time or to start a protest against you and eventually halt productivity. Yes, you have to listen, and you have to let them talk, but don't engage in useless, time-wasting debates that you've addressed 10 times before.

Don't go over your boss's head!

Overstepping the command chain to contact the "bigger" boss for an issue usually solved by your boss is a bad idea.

Your boss is your boss for a reason; this move will make your boss very annoyed. Unless your boss recommends that you talk to the big boss or for a serious harassment complaint, never make such a move. In doing so, you are underestimating your boss's authority and definitely, disrespecting him.

Compliments and rewards.

When you lead a group of people, part of your job is to delegate and give directives, and sometimes you have to "discipline" by applying your company's rules. But what is equally important and often neglected is the act of "compliments and rewards."

The act of "Compliments and rewards" diplomatically gets the job done and works precisely on "urging and pushing," but preferably called: "encouraging and motivating."

Inquire if your company engages in such exercises and apply it when it is due. A reward doesn't have to be expensive nor significant; your employees will mostly appreciate the gesture. There is a natural, equally positive, "psychologically-proven" human response to every positive gesture.

It shouldn't be material all the time. A word of encouragement, "thank you guys: thank God you work here," "You've worked hard today, your coffee on me," even if employees say no thanks, they will remember your acknowledgment for a long time, and next time you request anything, they will gladly do it.

Additionally, for your fellow supervisors or any person you deal with, a simple "Thank you." A word or two after an email, thanking them, or expressing: "how helpful it was"; I don't think you will ever meet anyone against that.

Most of your employees are one step ahead of you.
Watch for what you say.

You are one supervisor dealing with 25 employees, but they are separately 25 employees dealing with only you.

They watch you going and coming, sitting on your desk; they know when you depart for meetings and reports, arriving from lunches and breaks, and frankly, they know your every move.

And guess what, they adjust their every move accordingly.

You can't keep them all under your supervision continuously. And you can't be everywhere at once.

Most employees take note:

- When you are in a bad or a good mood.
- Of your whereabouts in any given hour.
- When you are tired.
- When you are in disagreement with your boss or with another supervisor.
- When you are extremely busy.
- When you are sick but still working.
- Of what other supervisors say about you.

And they can easily use these patterns to their advantage. They sometimes "pour gas on the fire" when they notice disagreement among supervisors. And they sometimes abuse your "busy schedule" to demand things knowing that you will be saying "YES" "on the go." Most of the time, employees observe your mood for the day before they come and ask for favors.

My advice is to preserve your feelings and private life outside your job, and more importantly, keep your opinions about other people and your political views for yourself. The more you share about yourself, the more you give them ammunition against you.

With or without reason, I knew many supervisors who like to comment on any subject, give their opinion, and voluntarily give out a cheesy company secret just to prove a point. New supervisors do it to make friends and to break the ice. You don't have to; it's preferable to keep it semi-formal with your employees than to break the ice.

Remember, you aren't on the same level with your employees, and for many of them, what you say with fun, they grab with all seriousness and hold on to it for the right time. Since their work is their livelihood, everything they can hold on to may be used in the future when they feel that their work is at risk.

For this reason and many more, let your composure leads the way and keeps it strictly professional as much as you can. When faced with requests and comments, respond with calmness and professionalism. You don't have to answer every question on the spot; always respond by: "I'm busy now, I'll get back to you." Go and examine and research before you answer. Don't play their games, don't open the door for gossip and don't react to pressure, and always say: "I will get back to you."

Stop doing 3-4 things at a time.

When dealing with "more than one" issue at a time, our minds are never 100% focused on the current situation. When we are multitasking, we often find ourselves half listening and paying partial attention to the issues raised. Don't be proud of multitasking; you will lose your edge if you do it too much.

If there is one thing you can take from this book and apply right now: please keep a pen and paper in your pocket, and every morning starts a to-do list. Your daily tasks "plus" the random requests daily will shower over your head all day long, and the only solution is to write it down to remember.

Most supervisors start a task then stop halfway if someone asks them for another. Eventually, you will realize that you are running all day with unfinished tasks and unclosed files on your computer. It's tempting to be this person, but you should choose never to be like this. Start your day by writing out a list of tasks and gradually adding to it as your day progresses. Don't stop and then skip something halfway to do something else; instead, write the new requests down and then go on with what you were initially doing.

Again, try not to give definitive answers on the spot and always use this answer: "I will get back to you." Because, first, you must look at files and study the matter's records before any decision; second, you have something on hand, and you need to finish it first.

CONCLUSION

Supervision is a gratifying field that helps build character, strengthen the mental state, and increase your people's skills. It makes you more organized, sharper, and more able to understand the way people think and act.

By supervising people, you can become a better speaker, an instant leader, and a confident negotiator. A good supervisor can become a father figure to people double his age and an excellent example to those who seek his advice and guidance.

Many trust their supervisor at work with family secrets and personal issues and simply respond to his or her suggestions.

The job also teaches you when and how you say "NO" without feeling guilty. It will benefit you even outside your company when you have to take a stand on difficult life issues; you will be equipped with a strong character, fewer emotions, and more organization.

The job also will teach you to accept the reality that you "can't please everyone" and that there will be someone who doesn't like you, and you will be ok with it.

When you carry out your tasks as you ought to, you will be more than satisfied with the outcome on several ramifications; and you'll be convinced that you can hold the forte in the face of even more challenging scenarios and tougher situations.

A strong belief in your capabilities will unquestionably spill over to the image you portray of yourself. Your subordinates will begin to view you as strong, capable, and someone who is in charge, thus helping you gain the respect you have always desired to have from them.

TR. Sabra

Made in United States
North Haven, CT
29 December 2021

13851293R00052